ACCOUNTING LIFEPAC
ANALYZING & JOURNALIZING TRAI

OVERVIEW

LIFEPACS 1 and 2 gave you an overview of the accounting system, including preparing a beginning balance sheet, recording the opening entry in the journal and posting the opening entry to the ledger. This LIFEPAC® will take you a step further into the accounting process as you learn how to expand the accounting equation to include income statement items. You will also use the T account to analyze transactions into debits and credits. You will learn about the double-entry accounting system as you journalize, using the general journal.

OBJECTIVES

When you have completed this LIFEPAC you will be able to:

1. Define accounting terms associated with analyzing business transactions.
2. Identify accounting concepts.
3. Understand the expanded accounting equation.
4. Identify balance sheet items.
5. Identify income statement items.
6. Understand the process of analyzing transactions into debit and credit parts.
7. Use the T account to analyze business transactions, indicating which accounts are debited or credited.
8. Prove the debits and credits for each transaction.
9. Record transactions in the general journal.

VOCABULARY

Account – a record that summarizes all the characteristics of a single item of the equation.

Account Balance – the computed balance of an account after all debits and credits have been posted.

Account Title – the name given to any account.

Accounting Equation – a mathematical equation that illustrates the relationship between assets, liabilities and owner's equity (capital): Assets = Liabilities + Capital.

Asset – anything of value owned by a business.

Balance Sheet – a form that shows the financial position of a business on a specific date.

Chart of Accounts – a list of all accounts used by an entity indicating the identifying number, the account title and classification of each accounting equation item.

Chronological – in order by date.

Compound Entry – a journal entry that contains more than two accounts.

Contra Account – an account that has a negative effect on a controlling account.

Credit – refers to any entry made in the right-hand amount column.

Debit – refers to any entry made in the left-hand amount column.

Double-entry Accounting – each financial transaction has a double effect and is recorded so that the total of the debit amounts is always equal to the total of the credit amounts.

Entry – a transaction recorded in journal.

Expenses – the cost of goods and services used in the operation of a business.

General Ledger – contains all the accounts needed to prepare financial statements.

Income – the difference between revenue from the sale of goods and services and the expenses that come from operating the business and making the sales.

Income Statement – a financial statement that reports the revenue, expenses and net income or net loss of a business for a specific period of time.

Journal – a business form used for recording accounting information in chronological order with transactions analyzed in terms of the accounts to be debited and credited.

Journalizing – recording information in chronological order in the journal, using the source document as evidence of the business transaction.

Ledger – a group of accounts.

Opening an Account – writing the account name and number as the heading for the account.

Permanent Accounts – balance sheet accounts (assets, liabilities & capital) that provide data from one accounting period to the next.

Posting – the process of transferring the information from a journal entry to the ledger account.

Revenue – the increase in owner's equity caused by the inflow of assets from the sale of goods and services.

Source Document – a written or printed paper that provides evidence that a transaction occurred and gives the information needed to analyze the transaction; e.g., a purchase invoice, a check stub, a receipt, a memorandum, etc.

T Account – an accounting device used to analyze business transactions.

Temporary Accounts – accounts (such as Revenue and Expenses) that gather data for one accounting period only; accounts used to compute net income for each accounting period.

Transaction – changes the value of the assets, liabilities and capital of a business entity.

ACCOUNTING LIFEPAC 3
ANALYZING & JOURNALIZING TRANSACTIONS

CONTENTS

Author: **Daniel L. Ritzman, B.S.**

Editors: Alan Christopherson, M.S.

                     Jennifer L. Davis, B.S.

Alpha Omega Publications®

804 N. 2nd Ave. E., Rock Rapids, IA 51246-1759
© MM by Alpha Omega Publications, Inc. All rights reserved.
LIFEPAC is a registered trademark of Alpha Omega Publications, Inc.

SECTION I. ANALYZING TRANSACTIONS

Using the T Account

Any business transaction will change the balances of accounts in the accounting equation. Therefore, each transaction must be analyzed to determine how the account balances are changed. Transaction analysis is the first step in the financial process. The relationship between a T account and each single item of the accounting equation is shown below.

The Accounting Equation

ASSETS	LIABILITIES + CAPITAL
On the left side of the equation.	On the right side of the equation.

The T Account

LEFT SIDE	RIGHT SIDE
Debit Side	Credit Side
Assets have a normal debit balance.	Liabilities & Capital have a normal credit balance.

The left side of the T account is the **debit** side. The right side of the T account is the **credit** side. Amounts recorded on the left and right sides of a T account are called **debits** and **credits**, respectively.

Determining whether an increase in a single item is credit or debit depends on its classification. Items on the left side of the accounting equation are classified as **assets**. *Assets* have a normal *debit balance*, therefore *decreases* must be recorded on the opposite side or the *credit side*. Items recorded on the right side of the accounting equation are classified as liabilities and capital. Since **liabilities** and **capital** have a normal *credit balance*, *decreases* are recorded on the opposite side or *debit side*.

The following illustration shows the relationship between placement of assets, liabilities and owner's equity (capital) on the accounting equation and each account's normal balance side.

ASSETS	=	LIABILITIES + CAPITAL
Asset Accounts		**Liability Accounts**
Left Side (Debit) / **Right Side (Credit)**		**Left Side (Debit)** / **Right Side (Credit)**
Balance Side		Balance Side
		Owner's Capital Accounts
		Left Side (Debit) / **Right Side (Credit)**
		Balance Side

The effect debits and credits have on the balances of these accounts is shown below:

ASSETS	=	LIABILITIES + CAPITAL
Asset Accounts		**Capital Accounts**
Debits increase / Credits decrease		Debits decrease / Credits increase
		Liability Accounts
		Debits decrease / Credits increase

4

Transactions Affecting Balance Sheet Items

In LIFEPAC 2 you learned that the **chart of accounts** is a systematic method of identifying and classifying ledger accounts. The first digit of each account number in the chart of accounts denotes the *division*. The second and third digits denote the *position* of the account in the division.

Generally, blocks of numbers are assigned to various groups of accounts such as assets, liabilities and capital. For example:

Asset Accounts	110–199
Liability Accounts	210–299
Capital Accounts	310–399

Shown below is the chart of accounts for **John Jones Enterprises**. Two new divisions have been added: **Revenue** and **Expenses**. Their division in the chart of accounts numbering system is shown below:

Revenue Accounts	410–499
Expense Accounts	510–599

Revenue increases the owner's equity in a business, while expenses decrease the owner's equity. Revenue and expense accounts are explained in greater detail a little later in this LIFEPAC.

JOHN JONES ENTERPRISES
Chart of Accounts

Assets		Liabilities	
Cash	110	Accounts Payable	210
Supplies	120	**Capital**	
Prepaid Insurance	130	John Jones, Capital	310
Equipment	140	John Jones, Drawing	320
		Revenue	
		Sales	410
		Expenses	
		Advertising Expense	510
		Miscellaneous Expense	520
		Rent Expense	530
		Salary Expense	540
		Utilities Expense	550

Since business transactions change the balances of the accounts in the accounting equation, each transaction should be analyzed to see which account balances are changed and how they are changed.

When analyzing transactions affecting the balance sheet items (assets, liabilities and owner's equity), there are four questions that must be asked:

1. What accounts are affected?
2. What is the account classification?

5

3. How is the balance affected (increase or decrease)?

4. How is each amount entered in the T account?

Following are several transactions for John Jones Enterprises. Each transaction is analyzed by answering the above four questions. The effect on the T accounts is shown below the analysis. In the first transaction the owner, John Jones, invested additional capital in his business. Using the above questions we can analyze this transaction:

1. What accounts are affected? *Cash and John Jones, Capital*

2. What is the account classification? *Cash is an asset account and John Jones, Capital is a Capital account.*

3. How is the balance affected? *Cash is increased because the owner invested additional funds in the business and Capital is increased because the owner's equity is increased.*

4. How is each amount entered in the T account? *Cash is an asset account and it increases on the debit side. Capital is a capital account and it increases on the credit side.*

Transaction	Accounts Affected	Classification of Each Account	Changes in Account Balance	How Change is Entered
Received cash from owner John Jones as an investment, $6,000.00	Cash	Asset	Increase	Debit
	J. Jones, Capital	Capital	Increase	Credit

Cash   **110**

Debit: Increase	*Credit: Decrease*
6,000.00	
Balance Side	

John Jones, Capital   **310**

Debit: Decrease	*Credit: Increase*
	6,000.00
	Balance Side

Several transactions are analyzed in the following illustrations. Read through each transaction analysis carefully. Observe which accounts are affected, what type of accounts are involved, how they are affected, and how the change is entered.

Transaction	Accounts Affected	Classification of Each Account	Changes in Account Balance	How Change is Entered
Paid cash for supplies, $600.00	Supplies	Asset	Increase	Debit
	Cash	Asset	Decrease	Credit

Supplies   **120**

Debit: Increase	*Credit: Decrease*
600.00	
Balance Side	

Cash   **110**

Debit: Increase	*Credit: Decrease*
	600.00
	Balance Side

6

Transaction	Accounts Affected	Classification of Each Account	Changes in Account Balance	How Change is Entered
Paid cash for insurance, $1,500.00	Prepaid Insurance	Asset	Increase	Debit
	Cash	Asset	Decrease	Credit

Prepaid Insurance   130

Debit: Increase	Credit: Decrease
1,500.00	
Balance Side	

Cash   110

Debit: Increase	Credit: Decrease
	1,500.00
Balance Side	

Transaction	Accounts Affected	Classification of Each Account	Changes in Account Balance	How Change is Entered
Bought supplies on account, $50.00	Supplies	Asset	Increase	Debit
	Accounts Payable	Liability	Increase	Credit

Supplies   120

Debit: Increase	Credit: Decrease
50.00	
Balance Side	

Accounts Payable   210

Debit: Decrease	Credit: Increase
	50.00
	Balance Side

Transaction	Accounts Affected	Classification of Each Account	Changes in Account Balance	How Change is Entered
Paid cash on account, $25.00	Accounts Payable	Liability	Decrease	Debit
	Cash	Asset	Decrease	Credit

Accounts Payable   210

Debit: Decrease	Credit: Increase
25.00	
	Balance Side

Cash   110

Debit: Increase	Credit: Decrease
	25.00
Balance Side	

Transactions Affecting Income Statement Items

Revenue and **expenses** are items that are included on the **income statement** for a business. An income statement is a financial statement that reports the revenue, expenses and net income or net loss of a business for a specific period of time. Unlike the **permanent accounts** that appear on the balance sheet during every accounting period (assets, liabilities and capital), revenue and expense accounts are accounts used to compute the net income for one specific accounting period only and are closed out at the end of each accounting cycle. That is why they are classified as **temporary accounts**. Revenue *increases* capital while expenses *decrease* capital.

Each transaction involving revenue increases the owner's equity. The transactions to record these changes could be recorded directly in the capital account. However, this would make it difficult to sort the types of changes to the capital account. For instance, were increases to capital caused by additional investments by the owner or by revenue from sales? Were decreases to the capital account caused by expenses incurred in the operation of the business or by the owner's withdrawal of funds from the business? To avoid this problem, accountants set up a revenue account for each source of income and expense accounts for each type of business expense. By establishing separate revenue and expense accounts, the capital account reflects only the owner's investment plus a summary of transfers to that account.

The owner's capital account is located on the right side of the accounting equation; therefore, it has a normal credit balance. Since revenue increases capital, it also has a normal credit balance. The revenue account increases on the credit side and decreases on the debit side.

Daily operating expenses of a business decrease the owner's capital by decreasing the amount of cash available to the business (remember the accounting equation). All of these expenses could be recorded in the capital account. However, correct accounting procedure requires that each business record its expenses in a separate account, making it easier to determine the balance of each individual operating expense.

An operating expense decreases the value of the owner's equity or capital account. Because it decreases capital, the drawing account will have a normal debit balance (since the capital account decreases on the debit side).

Drawing (the account that records the owner's withdrawal of funds for personal use) decreases the value of the owner's equity or capital account. Because it decreases capital, the drawing account will have a normal debit balance (since the capital account decreases on the debit side).

Any account that decreases a control account (in this case, the owner's capital account) on a financial statement is known as a **contra account**. The drawing account is a contra capital account because it reduces the value of the owner's capital account.

The following illustration shows the relationship between placement of owner's capital, owner's drawing, revenue and expenses on the right side of the accounting equation under the owner's equity section.

OWNER'S EQUITY

Owner's Drawing Account

Left Side (Debit)	Right Side (Credit)
Balance Side	
+	−
INCREASE SIDE	DECREASE SIDE

Owner's Capital Account

Left Side (Debit)	Right Side (Credit)
	Balance Side
−	+
DECREASE SIDE	INCREASE SIDE

Expense Accounts

Left Side (Debit)	Right Side (Credit)
Balance Side	
+	−
INCREASE SIDE	DECREASE SIDE

Revenue Accounts

Left Side (Debit)	Right Side (Credit)
	Balance Side
−	+
DECREASE SIDE	INCREASE SIDE

The following transactions affect the income statement items (revenue and expenses). Study them carefully and answer the same four questions as before. Observe which accounts are affected, what type of accounts are involved, how they are affected, and how the change is entered.

Transaction	Accounts Affected	Classification of Each Account	Changes in Account Balance	How Change is Entered
Received cash from owner as an additional investment, $1,000.00	Cash	Asset	Increase	Debit
	J. Jones, Capital	Capital	Increase	Credit

Cash 110

Debit: Increase	Credit: Decrease
1,000.00	
Balance Side	

John Jones, Capital 310

Debit: Decrease	Credit: Increase
	1,000.00
	Balance Side

Transaction	Accounts Affected	Classification of Each Account	Changes in Account Balance	How Change is Entered
Received cash for daily sales, $2,100.00	Cash	Asset	Increase	Debit
	Sales	Revenue	Increase	Credit

Cash 110

Debit: Increase	Credit: Decrease
2,100.00	
Balance Side	

Sales 410

Debit: Decrease	Credit: Increase
	2,100.00
	Balance Side

Transaction	Accounts Affected	Classification of Each Account	Changes in Account Balance	How Change is Entered
Paid the rent for the month, $450.00	Rent Expense	Expense	Increase	Debit
	Cash	Asset	Decrease	Credit

Rent Expense 530

Debit: Increase	Credit: Decrease
450.00	
Balance Side	

Cash 110

Debit: Increase	Credit: Decrease
	450.00
	Balance Side

Transaction	Accounts Affected	Classification of Each Account	Changes in Account Balance	How Change is Entered
Owner withdrew $200.00 for personal use	J. Jones, Drawing	Capital (Contra)	Increase	Debit
	Cash	Asset	Decrease	Credit

John Jones, Drawing 320

Debit: Increase	Credit: Decrease
200.00	
Balance Side	

Cash 110

Debit: Increase	Credit: Decrease
	200.00
	Balance Side

Transaction	Accounts Affected	Classification of Each Account	Changes in Account Balance	How Change is Entered
Paid $25.00 cash for postage (Miscellaneous Expense)	Misc. Expense	Expense	Increase	Debit
	Cash	Asset	Decrease	Credit

Miscellaneous Expense	520		**Cash**	110
Debit: Increase	*Credit: Decrease*		*Debit: Increase*	*Credit: Decrease*
25.00				25.00
Balance Side			Balance Side	

Transaction	Accounts Affected	Classification of Each Account	Changes in Account Balance	How Change is Entered
Paid the phone bill $295.00 (Utilities Expense)	Utilities Expense	Expense	Increase	Debit
	Cash	Asset	Decrease	Credit

Utilities Expense	550		**Cash**	110
Debit: Increase	*Credit: Decrease*		*Debit: Increase*	*Credit: Decrease*
295.00				295.00
Balance Side			Balance Side	

Transaction Summary for John Jones Enterprises.

Transaction	Accounts Affected	Classification of Each Account	Changes in Account Balance		How Change is Entered	
			Increase	Decrease	Debit	Credit
Received cash from owner as an investment	Cash	Asset	✔		✔	
	J. Jones, Capital	Capital	✔			✔
Paid cash for supplies	Supplies	Asset	✔		✔	
	Cash	Asset		✔		✔
Paid cash for insurance	Prepaid Insurance	Asset	✔		✔	
	Cash	Asset		✔		✔
Bought supplies on account	Supplies	Asset	✔		✔	
	Accounts Payable	Liability	✔			✔
Paid cash on account	Accounts Payable	Liability		✔	✔	
	Cash	Asset		✔		✔
Received cash from owner as additional investment	Cash	Asset	✔		✔	
	J. Jones, Capital	Capital	✔			✔
Received cash from daily sales	Cash	Asset	✔		✔	
	Sales	Revenue	✔			✔
Paid cash for the monthly rent	Rent Expense	Expense	✔		✔	
	Cash	Asset		✔		✔
Owner withdrew cash for personal use	J. Jones, Drawing	Contra Capital	✔		✔	
	Cash	Asset		✔		✔
Paid cash for postage	Misc. Expense	Expense	✔		✔	
	Cash	Asset		✔		✔
Paid cash for the telephone bill	Utility Expense	Expense	✔		✔	
	Cash	Asset		✔		✔

POINT TO REMEMBER

Any account will increase on its balance side
and decrease on the opposite side.

Complete this activity.

James Smith owns and operates a video rental store called **Movie Time**. Movie Time uses the accounts shown below.

a. Label the *debit* and *credit* side of each T account.

b. Indicate the *balance side* of each T account.

c. Indicate the *increase* side and *decrease* side of each T account.

1.1
Cash

a.

b.

c.

1.2
Supplies

a.

b.

c.

1.3
Prepaid Insurance

a.

b.

c.

1.4
Accts. Pay./Fox Film Co.

a.

b.

c.

1.5
Accts. Pay./MGM Film Co.

a.

b.

c.

1.6
Accts. Pay./Mortgage Payable

a.

b.

c.

1.7
James Smith, Capital

a.

b.

c.

1.8
James Smith, Drawing

a.

b.

c.

1.9	Video Sales & Rental	1.10	Advertising Expense
a.		a.	
b.		b.	
c.		c.	

1.11	Miscellaneous Expense	1.12	Utilities Expense
a.		a.	
b.		b.	
c.		c.	

 Complete this activity.

Kathy Bates owns a business called **Kathy's Korner**. Kathy's Korner uses the following accounts:

Cash	Sales
Supplies	Advertising Expense
Prepaid Insurance	Miscellaneous Expense
Accounts Payable	Rent Expense
Kathy Bates, Capital	Utilities Expense
Kathy Bates, Drawing	

Transactions:

May 1   Received cash from owner as an investment, $6,500.00

2   Paid cash for insurance, $450.00

3   Paid cash for supplies, $75.00

6   Bought supplies on account, $100.00

7   Received cash from sales, $890.00

8   Paid cash for the electric bill (Utilities Expense), $125.00

9   Paid cash for advertising, $50.00

10   Paid cash on account, $35.00

11   Received cash from sales, $625.00

12   Paid cash for Miscellaneous Expense, $6.75

13   Paid cash to Kathy Bates for personal use, $150.00

14   Paid cash for rent, $350.00

Instructions:

1.13   Analyze each transaction. The first one has been done for you as an example.

NOTE: Remember that the *account that is to be debited* is to be listed first.

Trans Date	Accounts Affected	Account Classification	Normal Account Balance		Changes in Account Balance		How Change is Entered	
			Debit	Credit	Increase	Decrease	Debit	Credit
5-1	Cash	Asset	✔		✔		✔	
	K. Bates, Capital	Capital		✔	✔			✔

1.14   Using the forms below, prepare a T account for each account for **Kathy's Korner**.

1.15   Analyze each transaction into its debit and credit parts. Write the debit and credit amounts in the proper T account to show how each transaction changes account balances. NOTE: Write the date of the transaction in parentheses before each amount entered in the T accounts. The first one has been done for you as an example.

Cash

(5-1) 6500.00	

Kathy Bates, Capital

	(5-1) 6500.00

16

Complete this activity.

George Hand owns a business called **Hand Securities** which uses the following accounts:

Cash	Sales
Supplies	Advertising Expense
Prepaid Insurance	Miscellaneous Expense
Visa Credit Card (liability)	Rent Expense
MasterCard Credit Card (liability)	Transfer Fee Expense
George Hand, Capital	Utilities Expense
George Hand, Drawing	

Transactions:

March 1 Received cash from owner as an investment, $2,000.00

2 Bought supplies on account using the Visa credit card, $500.00

3 Paid cash for rent, $500.00

4 Received cash from sale of securities, $650.00

5 Paid cash on account to Visa credit card, $250.00

6 Paid cash for transfer fees, $90.00

7 Received cash from sales of securities, $500.00

8 Paid cash for supplies, $400.00

9 Paid cash for insurance, $350.00

10 Bought supplies on account using the MasterCard credit card, $60.00

11 Paid cash for supplies, $600.00

12 Received cash from sale of securities, $950.00

13 Paid cash for the phone bill (Utilities Expense), $95.00

14 Paid cash for advertising, $230.00

15 Paid cash for miscellaneous expense, $25.00

16 Received cash from sale of securities, $900.00

17 Paid cash to the owner for personal use, $800.00

18 Received cash from sale of securities, $900.00

Instructions:

1.16 Analyze each transaction, using the chart on the following page.

1.17 Prepare a T account for each account for **Hand Securities**. Write the name of each account on the T account forms provided on page 18.

1.18 Analyze each transaction into its debit and credit parts. Write the debit and credit amounts in the proper T account to show how each transaction changes account balances. NOTE: Write the date of the transaction in parentheses before each amount entered in the T accounts.

1.16

Trans Date	Accounts Affected	Account Classification	Normal Account Balance		Changes in Account Balance		How Change is Entered	
			Debit	Credit	Increase	Decrease	Debit	Credit

Complete the following activity.

Kay Black opened a real estate business, **Black Real Estate**. During part of the month of June she completed the transactions below. (NOTE: the first two transactions involve more than two accounts. This type of entry is known as a **compound entry**.)

June 1 Invested $52,000.00 cash and office equipment with a market value of $8,000.00 in her real estate agency (*Hint:* you must calculate the amount to be credited to Kay Black, Capital.)

2 Purchased an office building for $105,000.00, paying $45,000.00 cash and signing a note payable for the balance of $60,000.00

3 Paid cash for advertising, $3,000.00

4 Bought office supplies on account, $60.00

5 Paid cash for office equipment, $720.00

6 Paid cash for office salaries, $600.00

7 Received cash for commissions, $8,500.00

8 Paid cash for advertising, $150.00

9 Paid cash on account, $60.00

10 Completed an appraisal on account (Accounts Receivable), $210.00

11 Paid cash for office salaries, $600.00

12 Received cash on account from charge customer, $210.00

13 Paid owner cash for personal use, $1,500.00

Instructions:

1.19 Open the following T accounts:

Assets:	**Liabilities:**	**Revenue:**
Cash	Accounts Payable	Appraisal Fees
Accounts Receivable	Notes Payable	Commissions
Office Supplies	**Capital:**	**Expenses:**
Office Equipment	Kay Black, Capital	Advertising Expense
Office Building	Kay Black, Drawing	Office Salaries Expense

1.20 Record the transactions by entering debits and credits directly in the T accounts on the next page. Record the transaction date in parentheses to identify each transaction.

Summary

1. Ask yourself the following questions when analyzing transactions:
   a. What accounts are affected?
   b. What is the classification of each account?
   c. How are the balances changed (increased or decreased)?
   d. How is each amount entered in the T account?

2. The accounting equation is used to determine placement of the accounts.
   a. Assets are on the left side of the equation.
   b. Liabilities are on the right side of the equation.
   c. Owner's equity (capital) is on the right side of the equation.

3. The classification of the account determines the normal balance side.
   a. Assets are recorded on the left side of the accounting equation; therefore, all assets will have a normal debit balance.
   b. Liabilities are recorded on the right side of the accounting equation; therefore, all liabilities will have a normal credit balance.
   c. Owner's equity is recorded on the right side of the account equation; therefore, the owner's equity (capital) will have a normal credit balance.

4. Changing the balances of the accounts is illustrated by the accounting equation.
   a. Assets have a normal debit balance. To increase any asset, the amount must be entered on the left side or debit side of the account. To decrease any asset, the amount must be entered on the right side or credit side of the account.
   b. Liabilities have a normal credit balance. To increase any liability, the amount must be entered on the right side or credit side. To decrease any liability, the amount must be entered on the left side or debit side.
   c. Capital has a normal credit balance. To increase any owner's equity (capital), the amount must be entered on the ride side or credit side. To decrease owner's equity, the amount must be entered on the left side or debit side.

5. The capital account must show only the investments the owner has made and the transfer of the net profit or loss from his business enterprise. Therefore, it is necessary to set up more accounts as a subdivision of the capital account. These accounts are owner's drawing (contra capital), revenue and expenses.
   a. As a contra capital account, Drawing represents a decrease in the owner's equity because of withdrawals made by the proprietor for his personal expenses. These expenses are not related to the business; therefore, they are not listed among the accounts of the business and cannot be used to determine income or loss. The owner's drawing account has a normal debit balance.
   b. Revenue accounts represent income to the business. This business income will increase the value of the owner's equity. The capital account has a normal credit balance; therefore, any revenue account will also have a normal credit balance.
   c. Expense accounts represent expenditures by the business. These business expenses will decrease the value of the owner's equity. The capital account has a normal credit balance; therefore, any expense will have a normal debit balance. The effect of this balance represents a decrease in capital.

22

6. Use the T account to analyze each transaction.
    a. The left side is always the debit side of a T account.
    b. The right side is always the credit side of a T account.

 Review the material in this section in preparation for the Self Test. The Self Test will check your mastery of this particular section. The items missed on this Self Test will indicate specific areas where restudy is needed for mastery.

SELF TEST 1

Match the following accounting terms with their definitions (each answer, 3 points).

1.01 _____ balance sheet items

1.02 _____ income statement items

1.03 _____ Assets = Liabilities + Capital

1.04 _____ shows the financial position of a business on a specific date

1.05 _____ any entry made in the left-hand column

1.06 _____ an account that has a negative effect on a controlling account

1.07 _____ increase in owner's equity caused by sales

1.08 _____ any entry made in the right-hand column

1.09 _____ the cost of goods and services used in the operation of a business

1.010 _____ reports the revenue, expenses and net income or net loss of a business

a. expense

b. balance sheet

c. debit

d. revenue, expenses

e. assets, liabilities, capital

f. contra account

g. income statement

h. credit

i. accounting equation

j. revenue

Identify each of the following items with an *A, L, C, R* **or** *E* **to indicate whether they are an asset, liability, capital, revenue or expense account** (each answer, 2 points).

1.011 _____ accounts payable

1.012 _____ owner's equity

1.013 _____ a building

1.014 _____ store equipment

1.015 _____ mortgage payable

1.016 _____ supplies

1.017 _____ rent

1.018 _____ money owed to a creditor

1.019 _____ income from fees

1.020 _____ prepaid insurance

1.021 _____ John Jones, Drawing

1.022 _____ cash

1.023 _____ utilities

1.024 _____ sales

1.025 _____ office equipment

1.026 _____ accounts receivable

Write *Debit* **or** *Credit* **to indicate what kind of account balance these items have** (each answer, 2 points).

1.027 _____ asset account

1.028 _____ revenue account

1.029 _____ capital account

1.030 _____ expense account

1.031 _____ liability account

1.032 _____ drawing account

Identify the actions with either *Debit* **or** *Credit* (each answer, 2 points).

1.033 _____ increase a liability

1.034 _____ decrease in capital

1.035 _____ increase in assets

1.036 _____ decrease in assets

1.037 _____ increase in capital

1.038 _____ decrease in liabilities

1.039 _____ increase in revenue

1.040 _____ decrease in expenses

1.041 _____ increase in drawing

1.042 _____ decrease in revenue

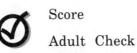
Score _____

Adult Check _____
Initial   Date

24

SECTION II. JOURNALIZING TRANSACTIONS

After analyzing each transaction into its debit and credit parts, the second step in the accounting sequence is **journalizing**.

The Purpose of a Journal. The **journal**, referred to as the book of original entry, is a day-by-day record illustrating the changes that occurred in specific ledger accounts because of business transactions. These entries occur in chronological order and contain the following information:

1. The date of the transaction.
2. The titles of the accounts affected: the account to be debited is listed first and the account to be credited is listed second.
3. The amounts of the debits and credits.
4. The **source document** number and/or a brief explanation.

At the appropriate time, the entries recorded in the journal are posted to the proper ledger account. These updated accounts are later used to complete the financial statements required by the business.

Although transactions can be entered directly into their accounts, it becomes difficult to trace transactions if errors are discovered or additional information is needed. It is important to be able to track each business transaction from the source document to the completion of all financial reports.

Advantages of Journalizing. The sources for organizing the journal are the business transactions. The source for ledger organization is the journal entry. By using both a journal system and a general ledger system, we increase the accuracy of the business records. Although it appears to create additional work, it has several advantages over directly recording from the source document to the ledger account.

1. The journal contains all the information about a business transaction in one place. Also, it provides a direct reference to the source document. The cross-reference to this document will explain the transaction.
2. The journal is a chronological record of all business transactions of that business.
3. Analyzing and then journalizing a transaction helps to eliminate errors.

Sorting the transaction into its debit and credit parts is known as an **entry**. With this information, a journalized transaction can be compared to the source document to verify the accuracy of the information. Another advantage of journalizing is that it keeps items in chronological order. Each transaction is recorded by date and, therefore, is traceable by date.

Recording the debit and credit part of each business transaction introduces an accounting system known as **double-entry accounting**. In a double-entry accounting system, each transaction affects at least two accounts, and recording the debit and credit for these accounts in the same journal entry insures that the debits and credits will be equal.

In LIFEPAC 2 you used a general journal to record the opening entry for a business. The general journal is the simplest type of journal and is arranged in such a way that it can be used for every business transaction.

Transaction Analysis and Journal Entries

TRANSACTION: May 1 – Received cash from Jane Howard as an investment in the business, $6,000.00, Receipt No. 1

Trans Date	Accounts Affected	Account Classification	Normal Account Balance		Changes in Account Balance		How Change is Entered	
			Debit	Credit	Increase	Decrease	Debit	Credit
5-1	Cash	Asset	✔		✔		✔	
	Jane Howard, Capital	Capital		✔	✔			✔

Cash	110	Jane Howard, Capital	310
6,000.00		6,000.00	

In the transaction above, the asset account Cash is *increased by a debit* of $6,000.00. The business now has $6,000.00 more cash than it had before May 1. The owner's capital account *increased by a credit* of $6,000.00. The owner now has a $6,000.00 equity in the business.

This is what the general journal entry would look like to record the above transaction:

	JOURNAL					Page 2	
Date 20—	Account Title and Explanation	Doc No.	Post. Ref.	General Debit		General Credit	
May 1	Cash			6000 00			
2 3	Jane Howard, Capital	R1		5		6000 00	
	4	6				5	

Journalizing regular transactions is only slightly different from recording the opening entry. In the opening entry, all the accounts with debit balances (assets) were recorded first, then the accounts with credit balances (liabilities and capital) were indented and listed next.

When recording regular transactions like the one above, use the following procedure:

1. If this is the first entry on the page, write the year in small figures at the top of the first column.

2. Write the month on the first line in the first column. You will not have to write the month or year again until the page changes.

3. Write the day of the transaction in the second column.

4. Write the name of the account to be debited under the account title column. Indent a few spaces and write the name of the account to be credited under the account title column.

5. Write the debit amount in the debit column opposite the name of the account debited. Write the credit amount in the credit column opposite the name of the account credited.

6. Write the source document number (in this case, *R1* for Receipt No. 1) in the document number column.

TRANSACTION: May 3 – Paid cash for supplies, $50.00, Check No. 1

Trans Date	Accounts Affected	Account Classification	Normal Account Balance		Changes in Account Balance		How Change is Entered	
			Debit	Credit	Increase	Decrease	Debit	Credit
5-3	Supplies	Asset	✔		✔		✔	
	Cash	Asset	✔			✔		✔

Supplies		Cash	
50.00			50.00

In the transaction above, the asset account Supplies is *increased by a debit* of $50.00. The business now has $50.00 more supplies than it had before May 3. The asset account Cash is *decreased by a credit* of $50.00. The business now has $50.00 less in cash than before because it bought supplies.

Since the general journal keeps a **chronological** record of transactions, the entry for this transaction is recorded *after* the May 1 transaction.

		JOURNAL					Page 2	
Date 20—	Account Title and Explanation		Doc No.	Post. Ref.	General Debit		General Credit	
May 1	Cash				6000	00		
	Jane Howard, Capital		R1				6000	00
3	Supplies				50	00		
	Cash		Ck 1				50	00

TRANSACTION: May 5 – Bought equipment on account from IBM Corporation, $7,500.00, Purchase invoice #6.

Trans Date	Accounts Affected	Account Classification	Normal Account Balance		Changes in Account Balance		How Change is Entered	
			Debit	Credit	Increase	Decrease	Debit	Credit
5-5	Equipment	Asset	✔		✔		✔	
	Accounts Payable	Liability		✔	✔			✔

Equipment		Accounts Payable	
7,500.00			7,500.00

27

In this transaction, the asset account Equipment is *increased by a debit* of $7,500. The business now owns a piece of equipment worth $7,500. The liability account Accounts Payable is *increased by a credit* of $7,500 because the business now owes $7,500 more than before.

NOTE: Since this business records very few purchases on account, it uses the purchase invoices instead of a special accounts payable ledger. However, if purchases on account are more frequent, it may become necessary to maintain a separate ledger for items bought in that manner.

The general journal entry to record equipment purchased on account is recorded after the May 3 transaction and looks like this:

JOURNAL							Page 2	
Date 20—	Account Title and Explanation	Doc No.	Post. Ref.	General Debit		General Credit		
May 1	Cash			6000	00			
	Jane Howard, Capital	R1				6000	00	
3	Supplies			50	00			
	Cash	Ck 1				50	00	
5	Equipment			7500	00			
	Accounts Payable	P6				7500	00	

TRANSACTION: May 8 – Paid $7,500.00 cash on account to IBM Corporation, Check No. 2.

Trans Date	Accounts Affected	Account Classification	Normal Account Balance		Changes in Account Balance		How Change is Entered	
			Debit	Credit	Increase	Decrease	Debit	Credit
5-8	Accounts Payable	Liability		✓		✓	✓	
	Cash	Asset	✓			✓		✓

Accounts Payable		Cash	
7,500.00			7,500.00

The liability account Accounts Payable is *decreased by a debit* of $7,500.00. The business now owes less money to its creditor. The asset account Cash is *decreased by a credit* of $7,500.00. The business has less cash available after paying the amount due. The journal entry to record this transaction is listed in chronological order on the following page.

ACCOUNTING

three

LIFEPAC TEST

102 / 127

Name _____

Date _____

Score _____

LIFEPAC TEST ACCOUNTING 3

PART I

Write the letter of the correct answer on the line (each answer 1 point).

1. To show a decrease in any asset on a T account, the entry must be made on the _____ .
    a. credit side
    b. dedit side
    c. balance side
    d. none of these

2. To show an increase in any liability on a T account, the entry must be made on the _____ .
    a. debit side
    b. credit side
    c. left side
    d. none of these

3. A revenue account's balance side is _____ .
    a. debit side
    b. credit side
    c. left side
    d. none of these

4. In a double-entry accounting system, debits must equal credits in _____ .
    a. a T account
    b. on the accounting equation's left side
    c. all transactions
    d. on the account equation's right side

5. The right side of any T account is the _____ .
    a. debit side
    b. balance side
    c. credit side
    d. none of these

6. To show a decrease in any liability on a T account, the entry must be made on the _____ .
    a. credit side
    b. debit side
    c. balance side
    d. none of these

7. The left side of any T account is the _____ .
    a. credit side
    b. balance side
    c. debit side
    d. none of these

8. To show an increase in any asset on a T account, the entry must be made on the _____ .
    a. debit side
    b. right side
    c. credit side
    d. none of these

9. The owner's capital account normal balance is _____ .
    a. left side
    b. credit side
    c. debit side
    d. none of these

10. The total amounts entered on an equation's left side and the total amounts entered on an equation's right side must be _____ .
    a. debits
    b. credits
    c. equal
    d. none of these

11. The normal balance of the owner's drawing account is _____ .
    a. debit
    b. right side
    c. credit
    d. none of these

1

12. The normal balance of any expense account is _____ .
   a. right side
   b. credit
   c. debit
   d. none of these

13. The month is written on any journal page _____ .
   a. in full for each entry
   b. for each entry
   c. once on a page
   d. none of these

14. As a journal page fills up except for a single line at the bottom of the page, _____ .
   a. the next entry is split between pages
   b. a new journal page is started
   c. entries are checked to insure debits equal credits
   d. none of these

15. Before each transaction is entered in a general journal, the transaction must be _____ .
   a. analyzed into debit and credit parts
   b. journalized
   c. placed on an accounting equation
   d. none of these

16. The source document number that is entered in the Doc. No. Column of any journal is a
   _____ .
   a. page number
   b. number assigned at the time an entry is recorded
   c. cross-reference from the journal to the source document
   d. none of these

17. Accounting procedures require that all words related to a transaction are _____ .
   a. written in full when space permits
   b. abbreviated whenever possible
   c. written above the line
   d. none of these

18. A memorandum issued as a source document includes a _____ .
   a. stub
   b. brief statement describing the transaction
   c. new balance
   d. none of these

19. An accountant has a choice of many different types of journals to use for a business. His journal selection is based on the _____ .
   a. nature and number of transactions
   b. total amount of sales for the month
   c. total expenses for the week
   d. none of these

20. When an error occurs in writing amount in the journal's amount column, _____ .
   a. the error is erased
   b. the error is erased and the correct amount is written in the column
   c. the error is erased and the amount is written in red
   d. none of these

21. When recording entries in a journal, the year is written _____ .
    a. in full for each entry   b. once on a page
    c. for each entry   d. none of these

22. Any journal with two amount columns in which all kinds of business transactions can be recorded is a _____ .
    a. general journal   b. a two-column journal
    c. a cash journal   d. a business diary

23. When a bookkeeper records the debit and credit parts of a transaction, he/she is _____ .
    a. analyzing a transaction   b. posting a transaction
    c. journalizing a transaction d. none of these

24. When cash is paid for an amount owed, the transaction causes _____ .
    a. a decrease in capital   b. a decrease in a liability
    c. a decrease in revenue   d. none of these

25. A device used to show only the debit and credit columns of any account is _____ .
    a. a real account   b. a general ledger
    c. T account   d. none of these

PART II

Complete this activity.

Sarah Clark owns a business called **Downtown Seamstress Co.** which uses the following accounts:

Cash	Sarah Clark, Capital	Miscellaneous Expense
Supplies	Sarah Clark, Drawing	Rent Expense
Prepaid Insurance	Sales	Repair Expense
Ross's Supply (creditor)	Advertising Expenses	Utilities Expense

26. Record the following transactions in the T accounts. Label each T account and record the transaction date and the debit or credit amount for each transaction.

Transactions:

January 1 The owner invested $1,000.00 to start the new business

2 Paid cash for supplies, $20.00

3 Received cash from sales, $115.00

4 Paid the January rent, $100.00

5 Bought supplies on account from Ross Supply Co., $70.00

6 Paid cash for repairs to the office door, $10.00

7 Paid cash for insurance, $30.00

8 Paid cash for stamps, $5.00 (Miscellaneous Expense)

9 Paid cash for the telephone bill (Utilities Expense), $15.00

10 Received cash from sales, $145.00

11 Paid cash for advertising in the local newspaper, $10.00

12 Paid cash to owner for personal use, $150.00

13 Paid cash on account to Ross Supply Co., $70.00

PART III

Complete the following activity.

27. Cody Williams owns a service business called **Williams Repairs** which uses the following accounts:

Cash	Blue Ridge Supply Co.	Advertising Expense
Supplies	(creditor)	Miscellaneous Expense
Prepaid Insurance	Cody Williams, Capital	Rent Expense
Equipment	Cody Williams, Drawing	Repairs Expense
	Sales	Utilities Expense

Instructions: Journalize the transactions completed during October of the current year in the general journal provided. Use page 1 of the journal.

Transactions:

Oct 1 The owner invested $7,000.00 cash to start his new business, R1

2 Paid cash for supplies, $250.00, Ck1

3 Paid the October rent, $700.00, Ck2

4 Bought supplies on account from Blue Ridge Supply Co., $900.00, P1

5 Paid cash for repairs to the computer, $50.00, Ck3

6 Paid cash for fire insurance, $1,000.00, Ck4

7 Received cash for weekly sales, $3,500.00, T7

8 Paid cash for advertising in the local newspaper, $75.00, Ck5

9 Paid cash to the owner for personal use, $250.00, Ck6

10 Paid cash to Blue Ridge Supply Co., $450.00, Ck7

11 Paid cash for stamps, $32.00, Ck8

12 Paid cash for a new computer for the business, $3,000.00, Ck9

JOURNAL

Date		Account Title and Explanation	Doc No.	Post. Ref.	General Debit		General Credit	

NOTES

JOURNAL

Date 20—		Account Title and Explanation	Doc No.	Post. Ref.	General Debit		General Credit	
May	1	Cash			6000	00		
		Jane Howard, Capital	R1				6000	00
	3	Supplies			50	00		
		Cash	Ck 1				50	00
	5	Equipment			7500	00		
		Accounts Payable	P6				7500	00
	8	Accounts Payable			7500	00		
		Cash	Ck 2				7500	00

TRANSACTION: May 9 – Paid cash for advertising in local newspaper, $55.00, Check No. 3.

Trans Date	Accounts Affected	Account Classification	Normal Account Balance		Changes in Account Balance		How Change is Entered	
			Debit	Credit	Increase	Decrease	Debit	Credit
5-9	Advertising Expense	Expense	✔		✔		✔	
	Cash	Asset	✔			✔		✔

Advertising Expense	Cash
55.00	55.00

Advertising Expense is *increased by a debit* of $55.00. The business has increased its operating expenses by advertising. The asset account Cash is *decreased by a credit* of $55.00. The business has less cash available after paying this expense.

The journal entry to record this transaction is shown on the following page.

JOURNAL

Date 20—		Account Title and Explanation	Doc No.	Post. Ref.	General Debit		General Credit	
May	1	Cash			6000	00		
		Jane Howard, Capital	R1				6000	00
	3	Supplies			50	00		
		Cash	Ck 1				50	00
	5	Equipment			7500	00		
		Accounts Payable	P6				7500	00
	8	Accounts Payable			7500	00		
		Cash	Ck 2				7500	00
	9	Advertising Expense			55	00		
		Cash	Ck 3				55	00

TRANSACTION: May 10 – Received cash from daily sales, $5,500.00, T10.

Trans Date	Accounts Affected	Account Classification	Normal Account Balance		Changes in Account Balance		How Change is Entered	
			Debit	Credit	Increase	Decrease	Debit	Credit
5-10	Cash	Asset	✔		✔		✔	
	Sales	Revenue		✔	✔			✔

Cash		Sales	
5,500.00			5,500.00

The asset account Cash is *increased by a debit* of $5,500.00. The business has increased the amount of cash available by taking in revenue from its business operations. The revenue account Sales is *increased by a credit* of $5,500.00.

NOTE: The source document for an entry of this kind can vary. In this case, *T10* refers to the cash register tape No. 10. At the end of the business day all the receipts that have been run through the cash register are totaled and the tape acts as the source document for total sales for the day. Businesses that do very few cash transactions may use a receipt book instead of a cash register.

The journal entry to record this transaction is shown on the following page.

JOURNAL

Date 20—		Account Title and Explanation	Doc No.	Post. Ref.	General Debit		General Credit	
May	1	Cash			6000	00		
		Jane Howard, Capital	R1				6000	00
	3	Supplies			50	00		
		Cash	Ck 1				50	00
	5	Equipment			7500	00		
		Accounts Payable	P6				7500	00
	8	Accounts Payable			7500	00		
		Cash	Ck 2				7500	00
	9	Advertising Expense			55	00		
		Cash	Ck 3				55	00
	10	Cash			5500	00		
		Sales	I10				5500	00

TRANSACTION: May 11 – The owner withdrew $500.00 for personal use, Check No. 4.

Trans Date	Accounts Affected	Account Classification	Normal Account Balance		Changes in Account Balance		How Change is Entered	
			Debit	Credit	Increase	Decrease	Debit	Credit
5-11	Jane Howard, Drawing	Contra Capital	✔		✔		✔	
	Cash	Asset	✔			✔		✔

Jane Howard, Drawing		Cash	
500.00			500.00

The contra equity account, Jane Howard, Drawing, is *increased by a debit* of $500.00. The owner has increased the amount of drawing she has taken from the business. The asset account Cash is *decreased by a credit* of $500.00. The business has less operating cash available.

The journal entry to record this transaction is shown on the next page.

JOURNAL

Date 20—		Account Title and Explanation	Doc No.	Post. Ref.	General Debit		General Credit	
May	1	Cash			6000	00		
		Jane Howard, Capital	R1				6000	00
	3	Supplies			50	00		
		Cash	Ck 1				50	00
	5	Equipment			7500	00		
		Accounts Payable	P6				7500	00
	8	Accounts Payable			7500	00		
		Cash	Ck 2				7500	00
	9	Advertising Expense			55	00		
		Cash	Ck 3				55	00
	10	Cash			5500	00		
		Sales	T10				5500	00
	11	Jane Howard, Drawing			500	00		
		Cash	Ck 4				500	00

Pay special attention to this next transaction—it affects more than just two accounts. This is a compound entry.

TRANSACTION: May 12 – Purchased a building for $38,000.00. The purchase price includes the building itself for $23,000.00, delivery equipment worth $10,000.00 and office equipment worth $5,000.00. Paid $4,000.00 in cash (Check No. 5) and has a note payable for the balance of $34,000.00.

Trans Date	Accounts Affected	Account Classification	Normal Account Balance		Changes in Account Balance		How Change is Entered	
			Debit	Credit	Increase	Decrease	Debit	Credit
5-12	Building	Asset	✔		✔		✔	
	Delivery Equip.	Asset	✔		✔		✔	
	Office Equip.	Asset	✔		✔		✔	
	Notes Payable	Liability		✔	✔			✔
	Cash	Asset	✔			✔		✔

Building	
23,000.00	

Cash	
	4,000.00

Delivery Equipment	
10,000.00	

Notes Payable	
	34,000.00

Office Equipment	
5,000.00	

The asset account Building is *increased by a debit* of $23,000.00; the asset account Delivery Equipment *increases by a debit* of $10,000.00; and the asset account Office Equipment *increases by a debit* of $5,000.00. These purchases show increases in the value of the assets owned by the business. The asset account Cash is *decreased by a credit* of $4,000.00 because less cash is available, and the liability account Notes Payable has *increased by a credit* of $34,000.00 because the business has increased its liabilities.

NOTE: Even though more than two accounts were affected by this transaction, the total debits still equal the total credits.

The journal entry to record the purchase of these assets and the additional indebtedness to the business is shown below:

Date 20—		Account Title and Explanation	Doc No.	Post. Ref.	General Debit		General Credit	
May	1	Cash			6000	00		
		Jane Howard, Capital	R1				6000	00
	3	Supplies			50	00		
		Cash	Ck 1				50	00
	5	Equipment			7500	00		
		Accounts Payable	P6				7500	00
	8	Accounts Payable			7500	00		
		Cash	Ck 2				7500	00
	9	Advertising Expense			55	00		
		Cash	Ck 3				55	00
	10	Cash			5500	00		
		Sales	I10				5500	00
	11	Jane Howard, Drawing			500	00		
		Cash	Ck 4				500	00
	12	Building			23000	00		
		Delivery Equipment			10000	00		
		Office Equipment			5000	00		
		Notes Payable					34000	00
		Cash	Ck 5				4000	00

JOURNAL   Page 2

TRANSACTION: May 13 – Sold merchandise on account, $1,200.00, sales invoice M2.

Trans Date	Accounts Affected	Account Classification	Normal Account Balance		Changes in Account Balance		How Change is Entered	
			Debit	Credit	Increase	Decrease	Debit	Credit
5-13	Accounts Receivable	Asset	✔		✔		✔	
	Sales	Revenue		✔	✔			✔

Accounts Receivable

1,200.00

Sales

1,200.00

The asset account Accounts Receivable is *increased by a debit* of $1,200.00. The business now has a customer who owes the business money, thus increasing the value of the assets of the business. The revenue account Sales is *increased by a credit* to indicate the increased revenue of the business.

NOTE: Since this business records very few sales on account, it uses the sales invoices instead of a special accounts receivable ledger. However, if sales on account are more frequent, it may become necessary to maintain a separate ledger for items sold on account.

The journal entry to record the May 13 sale of merchandise on account is shown below:

		JOURNAL					Page 2	
Date 20—		Account Title and Explanation	Doc No.	Post. Ref.	General Debit		General Credit	
May	1	Cash			6000	00		
		Jane Howard, Capital	R1				6000	00
	3	Supplies			50	00		
		Cash	Ck 1				50	00
	5	Equipment			7500	00		
		Accounts Payable	P6				7500	00
	8	Accounts Payable			7500	00		
		Cash	Ck 2				7500	00
	9	Advertising Expense			55	00		
		Cash	Ck 3				55	00
	10	Cash			5500	00		
		Sales	I10				5500	00
	11	Jane Howard, Drawing			500	00		
		Cash	Ck 4				500	00
	12	Building			23000	00		
		Delivery Equipment			10000	00		
		Office Equipment			5000	00		
		Notes Payable					34000	00
		Cash	Ck 5				4000	00
	13	Accounts Receivable			1200	00		
		Sales	M2				1200	00

Record these transactions in the general journal.

Josh Smith owns a cleaning service business called **Brooms-To-Go**. His business uses the following accounts:

Assets:
  Cash
  Supplies
  Prepaid Insurance
  Office Equipment

Liabilities:
  Jones Supply Co.

Capital:
  Josh Smith, Capital
  Josh Smith, Drawing

Revenue:
  Sales

Expenses:
  Advertising Expense
  Miscellaneous Expense
  Rent Expense
  Repair Expense
  Utilities Expense

Instructions:

2.1   Use page 1 of a general journal to journalize the following transactions completed during May of the current year. Remember that the first line of each entry is the account that will be debited. Source documents are abbreviated as follows: **Ck** (check); **P** (purchase invoice); **R** (receipt); **T** (cash register tape).

May 1 Received cash from owner as an investment, $14,000.00, R1

     3 Paid cash for insurance, $1,300.00, Ck1

     5 Bought supplies on account from Jones Supply Co., $1,400.00, P1

     5 Paid cash for rent, $750.00, Ck2

     7 Paid cash for miscellaneous expense, $5.00, Ck3

     8 Paid cash for supplies, $1,050.00, Ck4

     8 Received cash from sales, $650.00, T8

     9 Paid cash on account to Jones Supply Co., $1,400.00, Ck5

    10 Paid cash for repairs, $85.00, Ck6

    11 Paid cash for advertising, $110.00, Ck7

    12 Received cash from sales, $1,150.00, T12

    14 Paid cash for telephone bill, $75.00, Ck8

    14 Received cash from sales, $550.00, T14

    15 Paid cash to owner for personal use, $450.00, Ck9

    16 Received cash from sales, $675.00, T16

	JOURNAL						Page	
Date	Account Title and Explanation	Doc No.	Post. Ref.	General Debit		General Credit	

Record these transactions in the general journal.

Donna Jenkins owns a title searching service called **Title Search Unlimited**, which uses the following accounts.

Assets	**Liabilities**	**Revenue**
Cash	Office Max	Search Fees
Supplies	Wilson Supply House	**Expenses**
Prepaid Insurance	**Capital**	Advertising Expense
Office Equipment	Donna Jenkins, Capital	Miscellaneous Expense
	Donna Jenkins, Drawing	Rent Expense
		Repair Expense
		Utilities Expense

Instructions:

2.2   Use page 1 of a general journal to journalize the following transactions completed during June of the current year. Remember to list the debited account first. Source documents are abbreviated as follows: **Ck** (check); **P** (purchase invoice); **R** (receipt); **T** (calculator tape).

Transactions:

June   1 Received cash from the owner as an investment, $13,000.00, R1

2 Paid cash for rent, $950.00, Ck1

3 Bought supplies on account from Office Max, $3,000, P1

3 Paid cash for insurance, $3500.00, Ck2

6 Received cash from title searches, $1,500.00, T6

7 Paid cash for supplies, $650.00, Ck3

8 Paid cash on account to Office Max, $1,500.00, Ck4

9 Paid cash for repairs, $75.00, Ck5

10 Paid cash for the telephone bill, $110.00, Ck6

12 Received cash for title searches, $950.00, T12

13 Paid cash for miscellaneous expense, $35.00, Ck7

15 Paid cash to owner for personal use, $550.00, Ck8

16 Paid cash for office equipment, $975.00, Ck9

17 Received cash from title searches, $1,800.00, T17

19 Bought office equipment on account from Wilson Supply House, $3,800.00, P2

JOURNAL

Date		Account Title and Explanation	Doc No.	Post. Ref.	General Debit		General Credit	

Page

Record these transactions in the general journal.

Dustin's Service Co., owned by Dustin Harrison, uses the following accounts:

Assets	**Liabilities**	**Revenue**
Cash	Ceria Supply Co.	Service Sales
Supplies	Day's Equipment Supply Co.	**Expenses**
Prepaid Insurance	**Capital**	Advertising Expense
Equipment	Dustin Harrison, Capital	Miscellaneous Expense
	Dustin Harrison, Drawing	Rent Expense
		Repair Expense
		Salary Expense
		Utilities Expense

Instructions:

2.3   Use page 1 of a general journal to journalize the following transactions completed during June of the current year. Source documents are abbreviated as follows: **Ck** (check); **P** (purchase invoice); **R** (receipt); **T** (calculator tape).

June   1 Received cash from owner as an investment, $20,000.00, R1

2 Paid cash for rent, $900.00, Ck1

3 Paid cash for supplies, $1,600.00, Ck2

4 Bought equipment on account from Day's Equipment Supply Co., $18,000.00, P1

5 Paid cash for insurance, $600.00, Ck3

5 Received cash for services, $1,900.00, T5

8 Paid cash on account to Day's Equipment Supply Co., $1,200.00, Ck4

9 Paid cash for repairs, $65.00, Ck5

9 Paid cash for salaries, $789.00, Ck6

10 Bought supplies on account from Ceria Supply Co., $1,300.00, P2

10 Paid cash for advertising in the local newspaper, $75.00, Ck7

11 Paid cash to owner for personal use, $450.00, Ck8

2.4   Use page 2 of a general journal to journalize the rest of the transactions for June. *Hint:* Never split an entry between pages. Always make sure that the debit and credit parts of any entry are on the same page.

12 Paid cash for supplies, $980.00, Ck9

13 Received cash for services, $3,450.00, T13

13 Bought supplies on account Ceria Supply Co., $800.00, P3

14 Paid cash for Salaries, $989.00, Ck10

15 Paid cash on account to Day's Equipment Supply Co., $1,200.00, Ck11

16 Received cash for services, $3,590.00, T16

19 Paid on account to Ceria Supply Co., $1,300.00, Ck12

20 Paid cash for insurance, $1,210.00, Ck13

22 Paid cash for advertising, $85.00, Ck14

23 Paid cash to the owner for personal use, $550.00, Ck15

30 Paid cash for salaries, $780.00, Ck16

30 Paid cash for utilities, $56.00, Ck17

JOURNAL

Date	Account Title and Explanation	Doc No.	Post. Ref.	General Debit		General Credit	

JOURNAL

Page 2

Date	Account Title and Explanation	Doc No.	Post. Ref.	General Debit	General Credit

Summary

Analyzing Transactions. Analyzing transactions is the first step in the financial process.

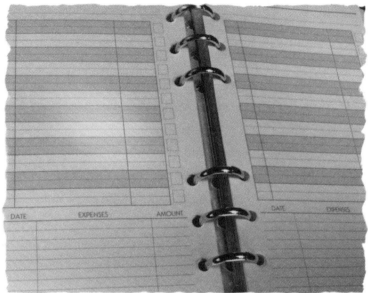

1. Analyze and record each transaction as increases and/or decreases in the accounts that make up the accounting equation.

2. A transaction will change at least two accounts in the accounting equation.

3. If a transaction causes changes on one side of the accounting equation, then increases on that side must be matched by decreases on the same side.

4. If a transaction causes an increase on one side of the accounting equation, then the other side of the equation must also be increased.

5. If a transaction causes a decrease on one side of the accounting equation, the other side of the equation must also be decreased.

6. Any transaction will result in at least one debit and one credit to the accounts affected by that transaction.

7. The debit and credit amounts in any given transaction should equal each other.

Rules for Debiting and Crediting. The type of balance an account has is directly related to its position in the accounting equation: Assets = Liabilities + Capital.

ASSETS: Since assets are on the left side of the accounting equation, they have a debit (left side) balance. *To increase an asset, debit the account. To decrease an asset, credit the account.*

LIABILITIES & CAPITAL: Liability and capital (owner's equity) accounts are on the right side of the accounting equation and have credit (right side) balances. *To increase a liability or capital account, credit the account. To decrease a liability or capital account, debit the account.*

REVENUE & EXPENSES: Revenue and expense accounts affect the owner's capital account. Revenue increases the owner's equity. Revenue accounts will, therefore, have a credit balance since increases to capital are recorded as credits. *To increase a revenue account, credit the account. To decrease a revenue account, debit the account.* Expenses decrease the owner's equity in a business and will have a debit balance. *To increase an expense account, debit the account. To decrease an expense account, credit the account.*

Journalizing Transactions. The second step in the financial process is to make a chronological record of all transactions in a journal. The journal sorts the information regarding each business transaction into its debit and credit parts. This is known as a double-entry accounting system.

Accounting Practices. Since the journal is a chronological record of all the transactions for a business during a specific period, there are several practices that must be observed when journal entries are made:

1. Errors are corrected in such a manner that anyone looking at a correction would understand what had taken place. To correct most errors, simply draw a line through the error and write the correction directly above it.

2. If an entire entry is found to be incorrect and it is discovered before another transaction has been recorded, cross out the entire entry and record the correct entry on the next lines of the journal.

3. If several transactions have been recorded before the incorrect entry is discovered, draw a line through the incorrect entry and write the correction directly above the error.

4. Dollar signs, decimals and commas are not used if transactions are recorded on ruled accounting paper.

5. Words describing the account title are written in full in any journal or ledger. However, if space does not permit, abbreviations can be used.

6. To avoid confusion at a later date, the cents column is always filled either with the actual money amount or two zeros if cents is not involved in the transaction. Do not use lines or dashes to indicate a zero amount in the cents column.

7. Neatness is important when completing any accounting information. Writing clearly avoids any misinterpretation of numbers or words at a later date.

Review the material in this section in preparation for the Self Test. This Self Test will check your mastery of this particular section as well as your knowledge of the previous section.

SELF TEST 2

Match the following accounting terms with their definitions (each answer, 3 points).

2.01 _____ "listed in order by date"

2.02 _____ accounts that provide data from one accounting period to the next

2.03 _____ an account that has a negative effect on a controlling account

2.04 _____ a journal entry that contains more than two accounts

2.05 _____ each financial transaction has a double effect

2.06 _____ records business transactions in chronological order

2.07 _____ an increase in owner's equity caused by sales

2.08 _____ accounts that gather data for one accounting period only

2.09 _____ the cost of goods and services used in the operation of a business

2.010 _____ reports the revenue, expenses and net income or net loss of a business

a. expenses

b. temporary accounts

c. journal

d. chronological

e. double-entry accounting

f. contra account

g. income statement

h. permanent accounts

i. compound entry

j. revenue

Complete the following journal entries (72 points).

William Morse owns a model train repair service called **Morse Trains**. Morse Trains uses the following accounts.

Assets:
Cash
Supplies
Prepaid Insurance
Equipment

Liabilities:
Lionel Trains
Webster Train Supply
Capital:
William Morse, Capital
William Morse, Drawing

Revenue:
Repair Fees
Expenses:
Advertising Expense
Miscellaneous Expense
Rent Expense
Repair Expense
Salary Expense
Utilities Expense

Instructions:

2.011 Use page 1 of a general journal to record the following transactions completed during June of the current year. Source documents are abbreviated as follows: **Ck** (check); **P** (purchase invoice); **R** (receipt); **T** (calculator tape).

  1 Received cash from owner as an investment, $19,000, R1

  2 Paid cash for rent, $1,900.00, Ck1

  3 Paid cash for supplies, $1,200.00, Ck2

  4 Bought equipment on account from Webster Train Supply Co., $1,000.00, P1

  5 Paid cash for insurance, $2,600.00, Ck3

  5 Received cash for train repairs, $2,900.00, T5

  8 Paid cash on account to Webster Train Supply Co., $1,000.00, Ck4

  9 Paid cash for repairs, $95.00, Ck5

  9 Paid cash for salaries, $1,789.00, Ck6

  10 Bought supplies on account from Lionel Train Co., $1,440.00, P2

  10 Paid cash for advertising in the local newspaper, $175.00, Ck7

  11 Paid cash to owner for personal use, $950.00, Ck8

2.012 On page 2, journalize the rest of the transactions for June of the current year.

  12 Paid cash for supplies, $80.00, Ck9

  13 Received cash for train repairs, $3,950.00, T13

  13 Bought supplies on account from Webster Train Supply Co., $1,800.00, P3

  14 Paid cash for salaries, $1,789.00, Ck10

  15 Paid cash on account to Lionel Train Co., $600.00, Ck11

  16 Received cash for train repairs, $2,190.00, T16

  20 Paid cash for insurance, $1,410.00, Ck12

  22 Paid cash for advertising, $285.00, Ck13

  23 Paid the owner cash for personal use, $650.00, Ck14

  30 Paid cash for salaries, $1,789.00, Ck15

  30 Paid cash for utilities, $560.00, Ck16

2.011

JOURNAL

Date		Account Title and Explanation	Doc No.	Post. Ref.	General Debit		General Credit	

JOURNAL

Date		Account Title and Explanation	Doc No.	Post. Ref.	General Debit		General Credit	

82 / 102

Score _____

Adult Check _____

Initial   Date

SECTION III. REVIEW & APPLICATION PROBLEMS

Summary

1. The basic accounting equation expresses the relationship between assets, liabilities and equity.

2. Assets are the economic resources controlled by a business entity and used to produce future growth.

3. Liabilities are the debts of a business entity.

4. Owner's equity (capital) is the financial interest remaining in the business after all liabilities are paid.

5. The first step in the financial process is transaction analysis.

6. These four questions must be asked in order to analyze a transaction: (1) What accounts are affected? (2) What is each account classification? (3) How are the balances affected? and (4) How must they be entered in the account?

7. If a transaction change occurs on both sides of the equation, both sides must either increase or decrease.

8. If transaction change occurs on one side of the equation, one account must increase and another account must decrease.

9. Transactions affecting an accounting equation item are analyzed in a device called a T account.

10. The left side of any T account is the *debit* side.

11. The right side of any T account is the *credit* side.

12. The account classification indicates the normal balance side.

13. The normal balance of account determines its increase side.

14. Any item appearing on the *left* side of the balance sheet equation has a normal balance on the left side (debit side); it is increased by placing the amount on the debit side and decreased by placing the amount on the right side (credit side).

15. Any item that appears on the *right* side of the balance sheet equation has a normal balance on the right side (credit side); it is increased by placing the amount on the credit side and decreased by placing the amount on the left side (debit side).

16. The rules of account analysis:

    Assets:

    Normal Balance: Debit Side (Debit Balance)
    Increases on the debit side
    Decreases on the credit side

    Liabilities:

    Normal Balance: Credit Side (Credit Balance)
    Increases on the credit side
    Decreases on the debit side

Owner's Equity:
> Normal Balance: Credit Side (Credit Balance)
> Increases on the credit side
> Decreases on the debit side

Revenue:
> Normal Balance: Credit Side (Credit Balance)
> Increases on the credit side
> Decreases on the debit side

Expenses:
> Normal Balance: Debit Side (Debit Balance)
> Increases on the debit side
> Decreases on the credit side

17. The second step in the financial process is journalizing.

18. The journal is referred to as the book of original entry.

19. A journal organizes all the information about a single transaction in one place.

20. All entries in any journal are recorded in chronological order.

21. Journalizing a business transaction helps eliminate errors in an accounting system.

22. Journalizing provides a direct reference to the source document.

23. Steps in journalizing:

   (a) Write the year in small figures at the top of the first column.

   (b) Write the month on the first line in the first column. You will not have to write the month or year again until the page changes.

   (c) Write the day of the transaction in the second column.

   (d) Write the name of the account to be debited under the account title column. Indent a few spaces and write the name of the account to be credited under the account title column.

   (e) Write the debit amount in the debit column opposite the name of the account debited. Write the credit amount in the credit column opposite the name of the account credited.

   (f) Write the source document number under the document number column.

 Complete the transaction analysis chart on the following page, using the transactions listed below.

3.1

   a. The owner, Jennifer Ryan, invested $50,000.00 in the business.

   b. Purchased a building for $150,000.00, obtaining a mortgage (Mortgage Payable) for the entire amount.

   c. Total sales for the week, $1,200.00

   d. Paid the rent for the current month, $600.00

   e. Paid cash for supplies, $250.00

f. The owner withdrew $550.00 cash for personal use.

g. Bought supplies on account, $890.00

h. Purchased insurance for cash, $1,200.00

i. Total sales for the week, $1,800.00

j. Paid cash for repairs to the delivery truck, $600.00

k. Paid cash for advertising, $250.00

l. Paid on account for supplies purchased, $890.00

Trans.	Accounts Affected	Account Classification	Normal Account Balance		Changes in Account Balance		How Change is Entered	
			Debit	Credit	Increase	Decrease	Debit	Credit
a.								
b.								
c.								
d.								
e.								
f.								
g.								
h.								
i.								
j.								
k.								
l.								

Record these transactions in the general journal.

Carlson Black opened a real estate business. Mr. Black uses the following accounts.

Assets
Cash
Accounts Receivable
Office Supplies
Office Equipment
Automobile
Land
Building

Liabilities
Accounts Payable
Notes Payable

Capital
Carlson Black, Capital
Carlson Black, Drawing

Revenue
Commissions
Appraisal Fees

Expenses
Advertising Expense
Miscellaneous Expense
Salary Expense

3.2   .Use page 1 of the general journal on the next page to record the following transactions for April of the current year. Source documents are abbreviated as follows: **Ck** (check); **M** (memorandum); **P** (purchase invoice); **R** (receipt).

Transactions:

April   1   Invested $38,000.00 in cash and $10,000.00 in office equipment to start a real estate agency, R1

     2   Purchased land worth $32,000.00 and a small office building valued at $100,000.00, paying $33,000 cash and signing a note to pay the balance over five years (Notes Payable), Ck100

     3   Bought office supplies on account, $75.00, P2

     4   Purchased an automobile for the business, $7,500.00, Ck101

     5   Paid office salaries, $600.00, Ck102

     6   Sold a piece of property and was paid $8,700.00 commission, R2

     7   Paid $250.00 for advertising in a local trade publication, Ck103

     8   Paid $75.00 on account for supplies purchased on April 3, Ck104

     9   Bought a new computer on account for the office, $1,840.00, P3

    10   Completed an appraisal on account and billed the client (Accounts Receivable) $210.00, M1

    11   Paid office salaries, $640.00, Ckl05

    12   Received on account, $210.00 from client billed on April 10, R3

    13   Mr. Black withdrew $1,500.00 for personal use, Ck106

JOURNAL

Page

Date	Account Title and Explanation	Doc No.	Post. Ref.	General Debit	General Credit

Complete this activity.

George Sims opened the following T accounts: **Cash**; **Office Supplies**; **Prepaid Insurance**; **Equipment**; **George Sims, Capital**; **Commissions**; **Rent Expense**; and **Travel Expense**.

3.3 Open the T accounts and record these transactions directly into the T accounts by entering the appropriate debits and credits. Use the transaction's letter to identify each debit and credit.

A. George Sims invested $30,000.00 in the business.

B. Purchased an automobile for $15,000.00 (Equipment)

C. Paid the rent, $1,500.00

D. Earned a commission, $6,000.00

E. Purchased office supplies, $600.00

F. Purchased an insurance policy for the business, $1,800.00

G. Paid expenses for a business trip, $680.00

Journalize the following transactions (50 points: correct month/year, 2 points; each correct entry, 6 points).

The business uses the following accounts:

Cash	Notes Payable	Revenue
Office Supplies	Kay Clark, Capital	Commissions
	Kay Clark, Drawing	Utilities Expense

Use **page 4** of a general journal to record the following transactions for the current year:

April	22	Received $1,900.00 in commissions, R1
	23	Paid cash for office supplies, $1,000.00, Ck101
	24	Received $2,500 as an additional investment from Kay Clark, owner, R2
	25	Paid the electric bill, $640.00, Ck102
	26	Borrowed $6,000.00 on a note payable, M1
	27	The owner withdrew $600.00 for personal use, Ck103
	28	Received $750.00 in commissions, R3
	30	Paid the phone bill, $78.00, Ck104

JOURNAL

Date	Account Title and Explanation	Doc No.	Post. Ref.	General Debit		General Credit	

Extra form:

Trans.	Accounts Affected	Account Classification	Normal Account Balance		Changes in Account Balance		How Change is Entered	
			Debit	Credit	Increase	Decrease	Debit	Credit
a.								
b.								
c.								
d.								
e.								
f.								
g.								
h.								
i.								
j.								
k.								
l.								

Extra form:

		JOURNAL					Page	
Date	Account Title and Explanation	Doc No.	Post. Ref.	General Debit		General Credit		